The Origin of the World

Other Books by Lewis Warsh

Poetry
The Suicide Rates (1967)
Highjacking (1968)
Moving Through Air (1968)
Chicago, with Tom Clark (1969)
Dreaming As One (1971)
Long Distance (1971)
Immediate Surrounding (1974)
Today (1974)
Blue Heaven (1977)
Hives (1978)
Methods of Birth Control (1983)
The Corset (1986)
Information from the Surface of Venus (1987)
Avenue of Escape (1995)
Private Agenda, with Pamela Lawton (1996)

Fiction
Agnes & Sally (1984)
A Free Man (1991)
Money Under the Table (1997)
Touch of the Whip (2001)

Autobiography
Part of My History (1972)
The Maharajah's Son (1978)
Bustin's Island '68 (1996)

Translation
Night of Loveless Nights by Robert Desnos (1973)

Editor
Angel Hair Sleeps With a Boy In My Head,
with Anne Waldman (2001)

THE ORIGIN OF THE WORLD

Lewis Warsh

ELLENVILLE PUBLIC LIBRARY
40 CENTER STREET
ELLENVILLE NY 12428

A Donald Ellis Book

CREATIVE ARTS BOOK COMPANY
Berkeley, California

Copyright © 2001 by Lewis Warsh
Cover collage by Lewis Warsh
Cover design by Wayne Pope

No part of this book may be reproduced in any manner without written permission from the publisher, except in brief quotations used in articles or reviews.

Some of these poems first appeared in *Broadway: An Anthology of Poets and Painters*, *Long News*, *The World*, *Shiny*, *Prosaida*, *Talisman*, *Gas*, *Skanky Possum*, *Downtown Brooklyn*, *Transfer* and *The Germ*.

The Origin of the World is published by Donald S. Ellis and distributed by Creative Arts Book Company

For information contact:
Creative Arts Book Company
833 Bancroft Way
Berkeley, California 94710
1-800-848-7789

Printed in Canada

ISBN 0-88739-343-8
Library of Congress Catalog Number 00-103038

Thanks to Wang Ping, Marie Warsh, Barbara Henning, Steve Clay, Sophia Warsh, Ed Friedman, Ed Foster, Gary Lenhart, Charles North, Bernadette Mayer, Max Warsh, Pamela Lawton, Rackstraw Downes, Bill Kushner, Mushka Kochan and Eric Malone.

Special thanks to Gloria Frym, who made the book happen, and to Don Ellis, publisher of Creative Arts.

CONTENTS

The Outer Banks	1
Entering Night	7
Avenue of Escape	13
Elective Surgery	19
Anyone But You	24
Invasion of Privacy	29
More Than You Know	34
Work in Progress	40
False Start	46
Sunday	50
Avenue X	55
Eye Contact	60
Polygraph	65
A Hunger Artist	70
Pirate Radio	76
The Origin of the World	81
The Secret Police	87

The Origin of the World

THE OUTER BANKS

You could say that characters in The Bible were obsessed
    with hiding their nakedness

I touch the leg of the table with the toe of my foot

The child searches in a drawer for the damaged toy

Feelings of love were impaired by excessive anxiety

I put in my order for the butcher before it gets too late
    & the holidays are "upon us" or so they say

You can wear the same clothing every day & no one cares

She complains that she spends too much time making herself
    beautiful while he just picks up the clothing he
    wore yesterday from the floor & doesn't even
    bother washing his face or combing his hair

I hear a rooster cry at dawn from someone's roof

I experience an epiphany, I'm not what you might call handy

There's a dead seal on the beach & a fishing boat
    on the horizon

The guy downstairs complains about a leak when I take a shower

Some people don't mind if you take them for granted

She can't break up with her boyfriend until she knows
    she has another waiting in the wings

It's hard to love anyone who holds a grudge

I wear my compromises over my mask

My deficiencies won't add up, no ice no drink

The shades of night toss their dilapidated forms over my shoulders like a Ukrainian shawl

Women with kerchiefs, a family with stroller, her equestrian thoughts ride into the sunset

Think of A's love for B in terms of the needs of A for whom B provides the promise of immediate gratification

The sun goes down in my mirror where I address myself not as "I" but as a you who exists outside me & can't think

I thought I'd take time out from my work to make a call but as soon as I heard her voice I hung up

A 16-year old student has been charged as an adult with attempted murder & unlawful use of a weapon in the shooting of a teacher who ordered him to stop smoking

Seek out a stranger to alleviate desire but don't call her back—she might be "busy tonight"

It seems like you might as well have a drink to loosen you up

In the summer of 1964 I lived in a bungalow in Far Rockaway with my girlfriend, her father & her baby

"She's not here now—she's never here—who should I say
   called?"

It strikes me: it strikes me that I repeat everything twice in
   my life, & keep repeating, without acknowledging my
   mistakes

Some people keep love at a distance because they're frightened of
   being hurt but it's hard to be on the outside looking in at
   your own life or perpetually standing on the edge of
   things with no where to go

We thought the matinee began at 3 but when we arrived it was
   intermission

People meet on a blind date & eventually get married for the sake
   of discretion ("my parents wanted me to")

You find out what interests you, but don't do it—not yet,
   anyway—since it's more interesting to put it all off
   till tomorrow, to let things slide, to trap the thought
   in its beauty like a tiger in a cage & watch it climb the
   walls & disfigure itself out of sheer helplessness

You map out a theory of knowledge & watch it dissolve like an
   integer divided by itself, but turned on their sides
   the numbers look like songs

You pretend to work hard so others will leave you alone

You talk to strangers & megalomaniacs, you read books you
   read before

You prefer pieces of paper with words on them to people, but
   that phase passes

You identify with the tree outside your window: all my family
   makes a home here but the branches are obscure, even
   to me

You sing a judicious symphony like a necklace of amber beads

A half-dressed man leans out the window & shouts to his
   girlfriend on the sidewalk

A police car with a loud speaker announces a reward for any
   information leading to the arrest & conviction of a person
   who shot a policeman

I was working in the library at Columbia University & we met
   during my lunch hour on the steps of Grant's Tomb

Tumblers on the tray bisect the light of the immigrant wafer
   which we place on the tongue to taste the snow, the rain
   & the spray which from yonder fountain alights on our
   faces

There's a bracelet close to her skin that resembles ivy but if
   I touch it I fear my heart might grow numb

The specialty of the house wasn't on the menu but you could
   request it from the waiter, the waitress or maitre d' who
   would bow down & kiss your knees out of a desire to
   give pleasure

Love is no solution to fear, the touch of a hand in the dark,
   nor the flowers, nor the beating of the wings against
   the screen

A job that represses your sexual instincts may be just what
   you need

"Don't wait up for me" is something I might have said
   but when I returned the bed was a talisman
   of crumbs & plaster

They say there was a lot of rain & possible flooding before
   we came: they tell us we brought the bad weather with us

Tell us what remains of desire, as you know it

All the swings in the park are taken, all the benches broken,
   let's sit here

There's a jail across the border where they'll take us when
   we get out of hand & from which we can see the evening
   star, a symbol of the persistence of desire

All they can do is torture us, behold us in wonder at our
   beauty, desiring to subjugate us because we're so unlike
   them in our sweet ways, & even our most muddled
   intuitions are wiser than the vows of militancy
   they concoct

I go to the prison of the practical world to take care of
   business

I look up my name in the index but it isn't listed

She was born & died before my time but if she were alive
   today we might have been pals

Bodies intermingle in a subway car—I stare covertly at legs,
   arms, eyes

I collect the wood & light the coals, but the wood is wet & I
   have to use a whole box of blue tips just to keep
   it going

I plant the symbol of order, Neptune's trident, on the opposite
   side of the archipelago & set forth under warm skies to a
   new terrain, spellbound by the possibilities of the future
   & the shadows of the strange birds hanging motionless
   on the horizon, but I don't know the name of the boat
   I'm aboard—it's like a shadow of some other boat
   that went down in the storm off the Isle of Good Hope,
   where promises of love were made only to be broken
   the next day, where marriage vows were spoken
   in the shadows of an empty cathedral, where friends
   & relatives gathered to wish you well—could
   anyone of them, or you, predict
   this spell of cold weather
   we've been having recently?

All the objects in the world won't unlock the door to the
   present where daylight strips us of night's desire
   & a voice riding the airwaves whispers into the fog:
   Don't lose heart

When I close my eyes I can see the after-image of the light
   of the candle like the face in a dream, you are my
   shadow

ENTERING NIGHT

There are fences around churches to keep the agony from
    steeping

I wash the dishes by starlight, it's all I can do for today

You get the impression people are laughing at him behind his
    back & that he doesn't care

Some day I'll come back to this street & say: I used to live here

The American woman in the Japanese restaurant opened her
    blouse & massaged her breast as she talked to her
    boyfriend who slouched in his chair

Won't order any new food in restaurant for fear I won't like it—
    order only what I like, another ruined evening

They tell you it can't last because they don't want you to be
    happy, people are like that I'm afraid

Don't think I'm being withdrawn if I seek refuge in my private
    world

I used to play "Für Elise" but then I told my piano teacher
    that I wanted to play "popular" music so he brought
    me the score for "The King & I" & I quit taking lessons

All we could do when we got to the park was sit on the grass, eat
    sandwiches, play ball

& so much to say, how long can I linger over this letter, among
    the boxes of tea & sweeteners, don't take everything
    for yourself

Before putting on mascara comb through & separate eyelashes
with an old toothbrush

You could hope for an act of generosity that wasn't someone's
idea of a deal, an exchange over a counter for some
commodity like the elixir of life

I knew better than to think I'd debase my own feelings by letting
them stagnate like weeds at the bottom of a lake without
first tearing them up from the roots with my bare hands
& laying them down in a neat pile on the shore

I stand in the waves at Far Rockaway & in the little breakers
at Jones Beach & haunt the Russian restaurants &
tearooms beneath the el in Brighton & swear to myself
but I'm only a virgin in the shade of a tree on a blanket
with my parents

Tactics of evasion give rise to purity of experience

In many cases the petting is limited to simple kisses & caresses

I failed as a child & later with my lover I reached out for

We exist reciprocally in relation to ourselves & to one another,
but if you go too far away you might cry out "Mother,
I'm lost" & return to where you began, start again
with a new person

You might think this book contains everything I know, but
when you come to the end you say: he's never been
in love

To have the bodies of one's closest relations eaten by someone
else is not as good as eating them oneself

It's the light around the edges of the city not the innermost
   self which speaks of trial & error in the judicial sense
   where people are sent up the creek for so many years we
   can no longer recognize them when we see them on the
   street, alive & free

Sometimes he loses the thread of a thought & begins to mumble
   to himself regardless of whether he's talking to someone
   or he's alone, but we don't interrupt him: maybe he's
   talking about us?

He deports himself as if he had tenure, but he can be fired
   at a moment's notice

Guy in sauna says, "Give me a cigarette & a drink. What's all
   this health shit anyway?"

Mummified deity come unbound: a struggle with loss is your
   next obsession

Love isn't a person or a thing or an abstract noun meaning
   itself or its derivatives nor is it a person replacing
   an object which you might desire to sleep with, nor is
   it inanimate, this person, nor can it speak, this
   thing, nor can it return love, this harbinger, nor
   stand on a pedestal, this star

& if we had but time to waste, to get wasted, I'd tell you
   the story: I'd call you long distance

We can hum along with the song until the promise of pleasure
   relates to a pronoun which in turn takes the form of a
   person who isn't here

What you say about hell may be a fiction, but she still isn't here

Each step of the day is a dwelling place for memories that
   underline—some might say "amplify"—your present state,
   by enfolding it in rigorous ambivalence of who you've
   become, leaving no stone unturned to the light of day,
   no moment sacred, while establishing a link of certainty
   to the transience of the hours of solitude where thinking
   "goes on" invisibly as an experience of what remains, the
   imminent floundering about of everything, the fin of
   a fish in the ship's wake

You can say of omnipotence a psychiatrist's sanity was
   well-earned

My great grandfather spent most of his time in a synagogue on
   Pike Street

If poetry arises from some hiding place then I want to sit down
   & talk with that moral eunuch who envisioned the poem as
   a medium between the heart & the brain

An acre of refinement that glows around the border like the
   winning number in a drawing: there are no matching
   socks

I need your attention to appease my anger

People wet their beds when they sleep in a new place for
   the first time

Ideas attached to words look frail in comparison as if someone
   were suffering from the catarrh that was going around

I fastened on a vocation before I knew who I was (my
   identity is a function of my relations with others, not
   what I do)

She rings the downstairs buzzer—I let her in

Moths blew in through the holes in the screen & a sick child stirred in her sleep, this was pleasure

On Xmas Eve I hitched over Mt. Tam on the back of a motorcycle

In his lexicon, the word "bourgeoisie" is an object of fear

Leaning your chin on your hand can cause acne—if your hand is dirty

My father went into the hallway & began calling for the police to save him from my mother whom he didn't recognize & whom he thought wanted to murder him & steal his money

Ask someone for advice & he says "all she needs is affection"

She was so surprised to meet him she didn't notice he wasn't wearing his pants

It's time I look out the window, you pass this way, you say you came a long way for nothing: sticker affixed to appliance

He limits his experience to what he reads, but content intrudes: the radio, heat coming up through the pipes, the words of a song

I can't read the blackboard but I'm too vain to wear glasses

The winds of the gods blow their words in my face

I want to go to a restaurant where the waiters call me "comrade"

There's no risk if you know the results of what you do, no inner
    growth in which recourse to action leads to attrition, no
    flower so insular it can't command its own fee

You can open the tomb in my presence & find the eraser

I guess they better recruit some new players to replace the old
    ones who can barely get up the court on defense & tend
    to stand around & watch the trajectory of the ball
    in its arc as it leaves the hands of the opposing players

"Look," you said, at the seagull on the ledge, but when I turned
    it had flown away

You look like someone I used to know, expressing dismay at my
    pregnancy, maybe the weather

AVENUE OF ESCAPE

She pretends that she's kissing him but their lips never meet

The cop stopped us outside Alberqueque & we dropped our dope on the side of the road

I had a way of hinting at what I was feeling without coming out & saying it

My sister teaches me to dance the lindy

Many separations end in reconciliation, although many of these reconciliations will later give way to new separations

The guy who replaced him had no prior experience but was willing to work for less than minimum wage

I had an alibi for where I was on the night of August 28, 1985 but the police still subpoenaed me to give testimony at a closed hearing

We hire someone else, a third party, to do our dirty work

When I was thirteen I got up on a stage in a house of God (so-called) & sang a song whose meaning the meaning of which was in the inflections of the words

A 2-ton trailer truck overturned on the Belt Parkway causing a tie-up on the Gowanus Expressway

I sing the emphasis of sound to convey meaning to somebody

I go to the store to buy some scallions

The obsession with undoing the processes of the past, the past actions & thoughts, until they're null & void

Once I was a hysteric, now I'm an obsessive-compulsive

Tchaikovsky's 2nd Piano Concerto on the radio: I'm too lazy to turn the dial

I shared a hotel room in Barcelona with a guy I met on the train who washed his underwear in the sink while I slept

She was wearing flat shoes, a white turtleneck, & over the knee socks

They found out the result of the test: positive, positive, positive

It might be sad to note that there are instances when words correspond with reality, like the word "reality" when you speak it, & the clouds pass in front of the sun

We wanted to go to the movies but I couldn't find a parking space so we rented a movie at the video store & went home & watched it

All the roaches in the drawer are pregnant

The ancient cutting off the branch of the forget-me-not grows to fruition

You can sleep over on the couch if you don't want to go home alone

The girl said she saw the murder from the window of her
    apartment, but no one believed her because of her history
    of drug abuse

Nothing I do can make her happy

The restaurant turned me away because I wasn't wearing a jacket
    & tie

It wasn't as if I could tell what she was thinking, or wanted
    to, but it was like the sun had vanished behind a cloud,
    all the light faded from her eyes, & I didn't have to ask
    "What are you thinking?" or "What's wrong?", I could
    tell what was on her mind by the way she crossed her
    legs & tilted her head

The people who spoke out against his policy were confined to
    their cells

Three to five with time off for good behavior, twenty-five
    to life with no possibility of parole

Out the window, in a moving vehicle, thinking & reading

I may be old, but I'm still desirable

She told me she was pregnant, that I was the father, but that
    she was marrying someone else

The distance between stars can be measured in feet & inches

The prison warden's wife runs off with an ex-con

He smiled, & every tooth seemed to have a new meaning

There's no future in becoming something if you can't accept who
    you are in the present & realize that the person you're
    in the process of becoming is a close relation to the
    person you are now

The therapist adjusts her skirt over her knees

She was 8, he was 14, they met in the basement, she touched
    his penis

It doesn't take a genius to realize that combining strong
    analgesics with liquor in great quantities can bring
    hidden personality traits to the surface

He sat in a corner waiting for someone to notice him

The elevator in the lobby was filled with young doctors

I strain my neck staring at the ceiling of the Vatican

You can say I felt helpless, dependent, like a young child
    who just bit his tongue, but when someone paged for a
    doctor on the intercom I snapped to attention

No one suffering from minor trauma, no one climbing the walls

The Latin teacher accuses me of cheating on the final exam

I could tell what she was thinking by the way she looked at me
    as if I wasn't there

It wasn't my nature to depend on my family for salvation but
    if I ever became desperate I would wire them for some
    money

You can pay me back, without interest, a little at a time

The whole class was punished because one student was cheating

The guy at the next table raises his beer bottle in my direction: "Hey, Bro!"

"I don't think I want to win anything, I want to die unadorned"

The fighter in orange trunks shrugs his robe onto the carpet

It's no longer appropriate to mention our names in the same breath

An announcement for a tag sale tacked to the trunk of a tree

I remove her denim skirt, her basketball sneakers, her golf cap

Hold back real feelings so they exist in new form complicated by not 'exposing' them to reaction of someone who hates you

The matinee was no longer during the day, but after hours, when even the quietest street turned its back on tranquility

It's not just because we're human that we want to experience everything

Once they sat in a theater, alone in their heads

I say things out of nowhere to draw attention to myself, otherwise I am nowhere

You can let love die without anyone knowing it

There's a half-hour delay at the Lincoln & Holland Tunnels

The man at the entrance to the alley glanced over his shoulder as he buttoned his pants

ELECTIVE SURGERY

You think you can begin as if it were ten years ago & you were still that person

A woman turns her head to catch a glimpse of her former lover

I offer you the key to a city without words

The guy on trial for rape wears glasses to make him look studious

The policeman arrested the soldier for fondling a single parent

Sometimes I create an imaginary aisle in my mind: we're walking down it, arm in arm, into the sunlight outside the church

The woman who approached my car & asked for a light wasn't a prostitute

You can escape your responsibilities by going to the movies or getting drunk

She picked him up hitch-hiking & they lived together for three years

The only person's feelings that I'm hurting are my own

Spaces that are only a dream of space, clouds that change shape as they pass over the rooftops, flowers that speak in flower language

Procreation isn't the only reason for fucking

He escapes his responsibilities by thinking about the past

It's possible to walk into a bar, depressed & alone, & leave hours later with a new set of friends

She unzips her dress in front of an open window

Behind each window, behind every curtain, a person is dying or sleeping

There are people dying, even as we speak, while others are sleeping or in love

I can remember it all as if it happened yesterday: the kids running down the hill to the dock, the woman on water skis disappearing beneath the waves, the dead fish floating on the surface of the lake

The fish aren't large enough to eat so they throw them back in

We go down to the dock to feed bread crumbs to the fish

The words get lost in the shadow of the page

Let's fuck one last time before we're old & stupid

All he could see of her body was the neck & the ankles

I made the connection between the body of a woman & a country, my mother

I live inside the body of a woman who isn't my mother

There's this new country across the ocean that resembles my mother

Give me a ticket to the land of milk & honey

The I.R.S. writes me a letter saying I owe them $6,500.65

I was standing in front of the class with paint stains on my shoes

I thought I'd discovered a new country but it was the same old person, my mother

My brain is an airport with no departures, no goodbyes

You come up behind me & cover my eyes with your hands

He purges his emotions until one thing remains

He had lost so much weight I could encircle his upper arm with my hand

One shrinks from the ineffable as if to ward off a blow

Some idea of perfection but no sense of value, the perfect thought

Express & registered letters take longer than regular mail

A poem is more like a tree than a shoe

Tenderness was resurrected as a model of empathy

Our founding fathers in their undergarments on the pages of *Vogue*

I was lead to believe that the job was mine for the asking but when I showed up Monday morning they told me they had hired someone else

An usher leads us down the aisle to our seats

All I know of the song "Mr. Blue" are the words "I'm Mr. Blue"

I know the words of "I've Got A Lovely Bunch of Coconuts," but
no one asks me to sing it

The little room has a purpose the way Puritanism has a purpose
but we don't want to go into it & talk about sex, we
don't want to pay someone to sit on a bed &
talk about sex

There's a little anger lurking in the corner of my heart

From here, it looks like a scar where the road turns on the way
to oblivion

I have a relationship with someone other than myself

My father looks up at us & says: you're not my family

Until yesterday, the word "orderly" wasn't part of my vocabulary

A person I felt close to fades out of my life

The cautious parent takes his child to the infirmary

I grew addicted to the feeling of being needed

He called the suicide hot line but received a busy signal

All this could happen when you were still a virgin

The phone rang & some guy asked to speak to my daughter

I want to tell you something, but you have to promise not
   to repeat it

As we said goodbye I put my hand under her sweater under her
   coat

The fragrance of a flower charged with meaning

I cut myself shaving, but it was only an accident (nothing
   serious)

ANYONE BUT YOU

I went to pick berries on the road to oblivion

They call themselves Communists but all they want are dishwashers & big cars

A light without shadow generates an emotion without reserve

Members of the staff leave the institution after an 8-hour shift, but the inmates stay forever

He can ask someone for money without losing his self-respect

My mother didn't know what I wanted for my birthday, so she gave me some money

I put my money on Awe Inspiring but it came in last

Border violations between genres were reported by the authorities

Type poems on stencils, run them off on the mimeo machine, call up friends to help collate & staple, mail copies into the world

I have some knowledge of her but maybe I'm thinking of someone else

I think of what I'd say, what I could possibly say, if we ever met

The place becomes the words you use to describe it but your feelings about the place have a life of their own

At parties we went to the bedroom where the guests stashed their coats, locked the door, swept the coats onto the floor, & took off our clothes

I changed my religion to please her parents, but they still hated me

New words are needed to heal the rift

We avoid each other in the bookstore, we pretend we don't see each other, I think you must feel guilty for not answering my last letter, you don't realize how much I love you, your last book was great

There's a beach all for yourself with a sign that reads "No Trespassing" tacked to a tree

How fortunate we are to be separate from the sea at last (mer = sea, mère = mother)

Mansions where executives once lived with their families will be split into apartments for the families of the workers

The cab driver orders me out of his vehicle: I owe him 17 cents

I postpone pleasure so I can enjoy it more later, boredom of expectancy when no one comes

We go to her house & sit on the living room sofa while her parents sleep inside e.g. maybe tonight she'll let me put my hand inside her blouse

The desire for objectivity harbors the intrusion of jealousy

It seems like you might never stop loving her, & then you do

There's the movie theater where I saw *Rocco & His Brothers* (dubbed version), there's the schoolyard where I played "asses up"

In the fairy tale, a wedge of cheese falls from his beak into a puddle

We can't tell the players on the scorecards without sleeping with them

Last year at this time, or ten years ago, or twenty, a quarter century passes by as if it were a quarter hour, or a minute

When I was nine I hit a girl on the shoulder with a stone to get her attention

This house will never be empty of the torment of loving

We heard on the news that Deng Xiaoping had died, but it was only a rumor

"No sweat" one might say as the solution to anything

I took a special speech course in college because of my lisp

Madonna's "Like A Prayer" on radio in schoolyard: it's the first day of summer

We smoke a last cigarette together before changing the sheets

I can spend in 5 hours what it takes me 3 days to earn

The used car salesman told me that he had a Buick with 130,000 miles on it for $1,600 that ran like a dream

I was in bed with her, in a dream, and her husband came in &
    said: I'm going to shoot you

I return home even though I know she's in bed with someone else

I opened the door with my key but she had put the chain on
    before she went to bed

Five Cubans calling for the ouster of Castro handcuffed
    themselves to a railing inside the crown of The Statue
    of Liberty

You return home on a crowded subway late at night full of
    resentment

Employers not only refuse to take on employees past the age
    of 35 but hesitate to put their confidence in someone who
    has never been "permanently employed"

You light a thin cigarette & then put it out after taking
    one puff

You go out for a container of milk & slam the door behind you,
    you curse under your breath as you take out the garbage

The Story of O tells of love as well, but in a different light

I was standing on a platform in the 14th Street subway station
    when a guy pointed a gun at me & another guy pressed
    a gun against the side of my head & said to my
    girlfriend: "What's a chick like you doing with this
    faggot?"

The people in the cars wave at me as I walk across the bridge

I see myself crossing the bridge, I'm going back the way
   I came

It's too late for me, but maybe you can learn from my experience

She knew I was coming home some day, but she didn't know
   exactly when

There was a chain on the door but she didn't hear me when I
   called her name

You can't call him a "bachelor" or a "sadist" & expect me
   to know what he's like

The blue of the Gitames pack on the table in the stranger's
   apartment

Back in the village, in the presence of their weeping sisters,
   the Marines were humiliated by their instructors

I look up words in the Thesaurus to make my poems sound more
   interesting

He was fired on Tuesday, without notice, & we never saw him
   again

Saw an apartment on 13th Street, between 1st & A, three small
   rooms for $800, but didn't take it

INVASION OF PRIVACY

I look for her under every awning

By accident, I spill wine in her lap or bite her neck
    when she offers her cheek

I watch her cross the street, against the light, with her head
    inclined

I see her in the shadows of the branches at the close of day

We invent a new language just to say the simplest things

It's a kind of dream just to watch her walk away

"In my profession I'm dealing the whole time with people
    who have collapsed under the impossible demands
    for emotional expression"

It's impossible to describe something that doesn't exist

The men on the A train were coming home from work, the words
    "Sanitation Department" stitched on their shirt pockets,
    over their hearts

I suffer in silence rather than risk the chance of rejection

An empty bottle of soy sauce alongside a can of warm beer

The highway buckles under the heat of an illegal dump

A guy on the Acropolis asked if I ever heard of Rudy Nureyev

I buried the placenta in a plastic bag so the dogs wouldn't
 find it

The lack of a stimulant, lying in bed trying to read—no
 wonder I'm tired

I went with him to Union Square Park to buy some valium

The life of one person, not someone you know, at the expense
 of others—without being mercenary

How happy we were, briefly, driving over the mountain
 through the fog

You can hear her voice talking to you from the pages of
 her book

Some say that poetry's both a window & a mirror, but today
 it's like a chalice filled with light: who needs to write?

There's not much difference between the words "garbage"
 & "jewel"

I dreamed of a woman who was there when the dream ended

My heart does the thinking for me in this house of stilts,
 if you catch the drift

I get angry at my boss & take it out on my spouse

She was arrested for the first time at age 17 for propositioning
 an undercover agent on the corner of 42nd Street
 & 9th Avenue

You define yourself by the place where the mattress touches
 your spine

There's a photo of my sister & me taken in Pasadena, summer '65

Alcohol consumption is still a problem in the fraternity
   where last year a 17-year-old student died of an overdose

I make my entrance in a world of appearances: it's the last
   trace of vanity, what I look like in your eyes

A diamond-shaped sign, with no words on it, tells you to slow
   down

A square sign indicates that you're entering a school zone

Illiteracy is diminishing, but the words have no meanings

It's a romantic notion to think that words still have meanings

They boarded the ark in pairs: two breasts, two penises

A roach crawls out of the newspapers on top of the radiator

The reward for my all-night industriousness is to see the
   streetlights go out at 7 AM

Potency is the same as frigidity, if you want my opinion

She was singing her signature song, the one about a dog
   named "Blue"

I suspect that I will meet you at a quarter past 9 on the
   steps of the cathedral near the dull university

You'll never know the pride of the fratricide, or who suffers
   most, the antidote to the illusion, the veil of philosophy
   in the vale of suffering, a praxis of the "moment" where

love sings its own eulogy & one minute I'm in bed & who
with is still asleep & the next minute I'm riding uptown
on the A train, shoes wet & the lining of my coat
torn to shreds

Her voice is the sound of a wood thrush in the abyss

The babysitter asked me if I could wait downstairs until she
    was safely inside her apartment

I drove the babysitter down a deserted road & asked her to
    tell me when to stop, but she never did

She was babysitting for her niece & nephew & called & asked
    me to come over

There were children everywhere, some of them thrashing about
    on the floor as animals do, making noises to show
    they're in heat

Don't think I'd act differently if I didn't know your name

A man is swallowed up by an object which isn't a woman
    or another man

When she told me my problems "stemmed from childhood," I burst
    out laughing

I stand on the grass & watch him jog along the edge of
    the highway

Windows are painted on the sides of abandoned buildings

In the middle of the argument she put her hand through
    a French window

Before you were born you were sculpted to resemble this
 other person, but now you are being alive in the sound
 of your own voice

Sleep comes to those who let it be, in the loneliest time
 of November, & the windows were smashed

MORE THAN YOU KNOW

What I hold in my arms could slip away at any moment

She was wearing her heart on her sleeve, but I didn't notice it

Your symptoms will go away if you talk about what's bothering you

There's a relationship between monogamy & prostitution that's better left unsaid

People obsessed with sex aren't usually alcoholics

No actions are meaningful unless someone sees what you're doing

A turtle crawled across the highway & was hit by a car

It's still dark out when I drink my first cup of coffee

Occasionally my lover confuses me with her father

It was more than just the way the branches of the trees intertwined, but how a whole living being seemed to be rising from the ground

You can't have everything, or so they say, so I settled for a cattle prod & a bowl of prunes

Proust used to stay in this hotel when he was in town

I finished the poem & put it in my drawer without showing it to anyone

He bought a coffin for his wife while she was still alive

It might be possible to rent a BMW or a Volvo & drive
    through town without killing anyone

There's pleasure in creating something, whether anyone
    sees it or not

There are stalagmites, evoking pain, hanging from the wall
    of the cave

I took her for granted & she left me for a man ten years
    younger

The woman in the hotel room charged a hundred dollars for
    an hour of her company, not counting tips

Face inwards & see yourself looking out dismissively at others
    who can only see you for who you are at a distance

Don't be afraid of hurting my feelings by telling me
    you hate me

My napkin falls from my knees to the floor

A unique arrangement of parts creates an entity (but the whole
    is not the sum of its parts)

Sharp words on lips belie warm heart beneath rough exterior

It's the duty of the child to kill his or her parents
    before they grow old

I can't imagine writing without an audience

The phone rang at 2 AM but when I answered it the person
    hung up

I imagine him looking over my shoulder as I write

Whether I was your lover or someone else's doesn't matter

It's easier to think about someone else than about yourself

She opened the door & saw a dead rat on the bed

She found an earring under the pillowcase & called the cops

My closest friend calls to tell me he's lost his virginity

It's hard to imagine an 18-year-old girl will fall in
    love with a 60-year-old man

Strong emotions interrupt the flow of thought

He had a brief encounter in a barn with a girl who was
    milking a cow

We live in a time when each person might discover
    the perfect mate

In the past, she slapped his face when he tried to put his
    hand down the front of her blouse, but tonight
    she let him go all the way

She pushes the baby carriage up the steps of Grant's Tomb
    that's part of my history

There's shrapnel on my spine, my heart in fragments

It was happening under my own roof but I didn't know it
    until it was too late

They came to New York to feel a sense of belonging to
    something that doesn't exist

I want to find what's wanting, circumcised lips, indulge
    wants needs until I gain the periphery

The implication was that if she took off her dress no one
    would come

I was enamored of the spot where I first met you coming
    through the door in a yellow jumpsuit

What respite from thoughts of old age blur into memory
    without conviction

It's never too late to find out the reason why you're alive

You retire to the bedroom before the guests arrive
    & prepare the crabs

In this way we might learn to flirt & hug without sleeping
    together

I think it's important to experience the act of adultery
    at least once

There's always someone waiting in the wings to take your place

Some motif involving celibacy, gliding through the hall
    in a nun's habit, the disclaimer about celibacy, my
    sister undressing in the dark, sharing a room with
    my sister & watching her undress

I stand outside the video store waiting for something to happen

He was part of the triangle, on the side where the husband
    falls asleep in his lover's arms, or the wife asks
    him where he's been & he says: I went for a walk

These houses, with a dog barking behind every gate, are your
    prisons

She drove up to Boston & bought a handbag on sale at Filene's

Only from despair can we awaken with something cold on our
    tongues & our cheeks pressed against the stained glass
    window when no one's looking

I felt adventurous for a moment & boarded the plane to Athens

It's not uncommon to make love to one person while thinking
    about someone else

There's a garden of wildflowers where we can begin our
    lives over again if you want

We need a fresh start, our backs against the trunk of a tree

I was sorry to say that when I looked in the mirror I no
    longer recognized the person I'd become

We had a rendezvous on the steps leading to the garden
    but she never came

I keep the salt on top of the icebox along with honey
    & a bottle of cognac

A feeling of abandonment passes through the wall of sleep

It's possible to love someone more than yourself

All my relationships begin differently, but end in the same way

He returned home from Europe, put his key in the lock, & called her name

WORK IN PROGRESS

I dictate my letters to an attractive secretary named Babette

Lunch is served: soup with kumquats, mixed seafood grill with bouillabaisse sauce, root ravioli & chocolate chip cookies

There's a new restaurant open on 14th Street called Babette's

After the movies we go for a drink at Babette's

This place is sacred because a child was born in it

The house was haunted by the child who died in her crib

Tell all your friends about the new restaurant on 14th Street called Babette's

The husband returns home early from the party & assaults the babysitter

Everything you do is a crime in someone's eyes

I left the muffin in the toaster & the smoke alarm went off

He had an affair with his landlady to prove his virility

My phone number is in the Brooklyn phonebook under Marsh

My feelings are a function of how much I weigh

There's a need for a comprehensible, accurate, up-to-date discussion of cosmology which doesn't talk down to the lay reader

I move out of my house to make room for his clothes

She plays with her doll as if it were her baby

The book looked more interesting when I thumbed through it in
 the library than when I took it home but I read it anyway listening
 to the faucet

The doctor performs an autopsy on the body of the drowned prostitute

One could say "I love you" to a friend who would understand that
 you didn't mean it

How long can you stay on the threshold, in the place that joins one thing
 to another, without feeling the pain of exclusion & doubt

Long stretches of small talk fill our day

I point out the street where he can find a brothel

The man at the next table says "Ouch" when the waiter brings him
 his check

You can trip on a crack in the pavement or toss a baby into the air

I get out of bed only half-pissed off & huddle in corner only half-sober
 thoughts in head as I thought my body talked "I heard you light
 3 matches" the other said we stopped & I peed in the women's
 bathroom, the trees lacquered yellow & falling off from each
 branch

I pretend we're in the front seat of a car in a parking lot at a beach
 near the Long Island Sound, & you're giving me a—no, I can't say
 it—although I'm glad you're feeling happier today

The teacher who seduced her student received a life sentence
 without parole

It's possible to respond with a salutation or a coy remark that might be misconstrued as a gesture of narcissism or nostalgia

He sat at a bar & told his problems to a stranger

I'm just holding down the fort until the replacements can get here

My body walks faster than most cars & buses

Long-term relationships, like Dante & Lautreamont, are often more inspiring than 1-night stands

I won't write in my journal until I find my expensive pen

In a dispute between a tenured professor & an adjunct, the tenured professor is always wrong

I'd like you to do me a small favor but I don't know what it is

My idea of what I want to do right now is get a career that I love, like being a legal secretary or something

There's no border between an object & a person who thinks

I used to know what to do with myself when I was alone

He said he had the hots for something, not a person but some object that made him sweat whenever he saw it behind a plate glass window

I finish the novel & publish it the next day

You can say "it took my breath away" & I'll know what you mean

He swam to freedom across the MeKong River in his socks

Don't forget to lock the door & close the windows before you go out

The room was empty except for an usher in a uniform sweeping up
    cigarette butts & a young girl selling soft drinks behind a counter

We take off our clothes & go into the water, we swim in the nude
    but don't touch

I went over to her house on my lunch hour & never returned to my job

All the money in the world won't make me rat on my friends

It was late at night when he came home with an erection & went to bed

I'm not sure you can pay off your debts with words: "I still love you"
    or "I'll always love you" don't carry much weight around here

If you ever get sick or need help in an emergency, we're the people
    to call

There's a rumor that a shipment of bayonets is going to arrive in
    Bangkok in a couple of days

You can rationalize anger by saying it's better to feel hate than
    indifference

You can penetrate with words, too, words like "transient" & "deciduous,"
    by which we speak of the comings & goings of the leaves
    & the passage of seasons

She receives a suspended sentence for asking the author's intention

The father buys his son a bar of chocolate for the ride home

We're the dependable people, the ones who go swimming in the dark
    but don't touch

My son snapped on the TV to watch "Who's The Boss?"

I know if I put my mind to it I could lose a pound every hour

A life where no one says good morning, good night, goodbye

I made detours to make sure we'd meet one another on the way to class

There's the motor lodge in Santa Monica where we spent the night

She thought that posing nude for the magazine would help her career

There used to be a bookstore around here, where people drank coffee & smoked

I nudge the tip of your breast with the point of my elbow to get your attention

I thought about her during the day & dreamed about her at night

There's a plane leaving for Athens in twenty minutes: all aboard

I remember her brushing her hair as if it was yesterday

The only way to get his attention is to pretend that you're dying

I lost my virginity in this room, in this tree

They told me to take off my clothes, put on a gown, & get into bed

It wasn't as if someone had gotten pregnant without wanting to

I was lying in bed reading Whitehead while you were in the bathroom being sick

Thanks, doctor, for telling me what's wrong with my body

There used to be a restaurant around here, where you could sit for hours over a cup of coffee

It's possible to start a conversation with a stranger without the fear of being rejected

Women take relationships with children for granted because they give birth to them but men need to assert that relationship

I say the worst thing that comes into my head

My father might die without my seeing him

Magnolia blossoms blanket the floor of the garden

Fiction is generated by fading memories

Your hair stylist knows your hair better than anyone

He depleted his faculties by making excuses

I cast someone in my role but he flubs the lines

As much as one might want to get on with one's life, if one could

FALSE START

I open my mouth, as if to speak, & then close it, without saying anything

He sat up in his coffin & said: "Don't I know you?"

We stood on the street corner waiting for the firecrackers to go off

I remember her smile, as I led her across the dance floor, & the tears in her eyes when I stepped on her toes

A single drop of rain explodes on the windshield: my father drinks coffee from a red thermos to stay awake

She told me that her boyfriend put a cigarette out in the palm of his hand when she told him she never wanted to see him again

I've put off writing this because I don't know if words can convey what I'm feeling

The audience knew that the contestants had been given the answers ahead of time, but no one cared

I'd just as soon go down to the Seaport to watch the tall ships as lease a Honda

She was wearing white shoes, patent-leather, like ballet slippers, & had a corsage pinned to her dress

Something that happened to you when you were a child made you act the way you did

The woman directed the police to the place where the
    executive was buried

I raised my hand in class & when the teacher called on me I
    shook my head as if to imply that what I had wanted to
    say was no longer important

Every time I open a book, I see her face

I like to think I have a lot of faith in words, but it's not true

He connects each word to a single breath, like a kind of
    prayer, as if the air was filled with particles of the body of
    some deity he didn't know, & the air contained all the
    elements of that body as well

I thought I heard someone knocking at the door, but it was
    only the wind

She fell asleep in the front seat of the car, crumpled up in the
    corner like a doll who could defecate & breathe

The only word that comes close is "desire," but it's more than that

I decide to become an ombudsman because I like the word

The cat leaves a dead mole on the steps of the porch

She walked across the gymnasium & asked me if I wanted
    to dance

You look better in profile, thinking in reflections instead of
    words

I could smell the lighter fluid & the smoke from the
    barbecue in another garden

I create a person in my imagination who never existed before

Her mother answers the door in an embroidered slip

Against all grievances can I reduce one wafer of kindness in homage to a single memory left over from an indifferent childhood

The noon siren enthralls the workers in their cubicles

I can't read more than two or three pages in one sitting

I thought I could be in a room & no one would see me but now the room is spinning: where shall we go for dinner?

Everyone risks investment but love wasn't involved

I cross the room to where she's sitting at a table with her friends & ask her to dance

A dog licks my hand as a sign of affection in another life

There are magnetized letters on the door of the icebox, just like home

I cut the food into tiny pieces & arrange them on my father's plate

A young woman enters the clinic with a sore throat & a headache

Some former CIA agents & Vietnamese generals were having drinks together in the back of the bar

The only sex I remember took place in my head

A government carried on by the rich for their own interests

The present is like walking around inside a mirror but the
    past is always slipping away & then you're finding it

Unlike most girls she didn't push me away when I tried to put
    my hand down the front of her blouse

The alleged kidnappers were confined to their cells in the
    depth of the tombs for fear they might flee if set free on
    their own reconnaissance

There are terms like "being" and "living" which no longer apply

The woman undressing at the window seemed to know I was
    watching her

When the sun goes down we'll go outside for a look at the
    crabs on the beach

I can begin the story anywhere & it won't make a difference

It excited me to think that he was watching me undress—night
    after night—at the open window

My favorite novels are *Battle Cry, The Amboy Dukes, A Stone for
    Danny Fisher* and *The Hoods*

The mouth does the work that the hands were trained to do

The man at the garage charged me $450 for a rebuilt transmission

A slave doesn't have to worry about his or her job

"I'm going to put my uniform in the laundry," my son says

SUNDAY

Sunday is the day of the week characterized by monotony
    & boredom

A dejected husband pushes a baby carriage in the company of
    his disheveled wife

I wanted to tell you that I was pregnant but you weren't
    interested

I was frightened that if I told you I was pregnant again
    you might leave me for someone else

Whether you're for something or against it is the same thing

His goal was to grasp things in the mind "the way the penis
    is grasped by the vagina"

All genuine knowledge originates in direct experience

I talk to people who aren't real in my head

Whenever you label something you exclude it from reality

I was reduced to being the object of someone else's desire

On Sunday, she went for a walk in the park with her lover

She told her husband she was going to see her mother
    but she visited her lover instead

"A ruler's superiority over ordinary people should be shown
    not by weakness but endurance"

Knowing what ought to be done & doing the opposite

The man's orgasm puts an end to the woman's pleasure

In 1715 Daniel Fahrenheit invented the thermometer

Life equals animation of matter: 1600

"Life is the opposite of indifference to one's surroundings"

The heredity elements that combine during copulation
   (the elimination of the false by the true)

Some thoughts are prearranged like acorns around
   the trunk of a tree

It was a long time coming, someone sang, but now that it's here
   no one's interested

I'd bet a week's wages I can guess your mother's maiden name

You can't write without someone looking over your shoulder

I leaned forward so he could see down the front of my blouse

All I want to do is meet someone new whom I can talk to
   for a few minutes, & then goodbye

One of the victims alleged that the defendant made small
   incisions on her arm with a penknife

Everyone I pass on the street looks at me & smiles & it seems
   like I could have my pick of guys I'd want to sleep with but
   every night every night including Sunday I sleep alone

A tourist on a modest budget talks to a woman in a cafe

The frenzy of ecstasy is preferable to the pleasure of existing

The idea of dying for one's country never appealed to me

It's possible for rigor mortis to set in before you die

What I want to do is go up to a stranger & begin talking

There was no place to wash my hands so I wiped them on my pants

Use the metaphor of the body to describe something broken (use ellipsis marks to denote absence)

It wasn't until we were in bed together that I realized she was twice my age

The doctor, his receptionist, a vial of pills

Artaud called the Surrealists "toilet-paper revolutionaries"

The chronology of verification has its own viscosity

"I was a nobody until I met you & that's the truth"

Actually knowing something more than the time it takes to do something is no less breathtaking than accomplishing nothing

Misshapen tongue curls into unseemly holes

Alcohol, clear glass, paper, artillery, printing, the compass

Your name is on the bottom of my list but I haven't forgotten you

It's important not to fall down on the sidewalk if you want
    to make a good impression on your future employer

We left the restaurant with the geishas & climbed into the backseat
    of the limo

I was half-asleep when the phone rang, so I decided
    not to answer

The woman at the other end said I had called the wrong number

When I said she wasn't home, he hung up without leaving his name

The cherry picker gets into a truck with the words "Arbor Barber"
    on the side

The phrase "I'm old enough to be your father" comes into
    my head, but I don't say it

You told me that most students had fantasies about sleeping
    with their teachers

It was possible that you thought of me as your father,
    but your real father was still alive

A young man with bad teeth sits on the side of the bed

I bent down to pick up my daughter & threw out my back

He was having an orgasm but didn't know it

Kierkegaard took refuge in the god of Abraham

All dressed up (as usual) in your Nazi regalia, you go for a walk
    in the public square

An antidote is a correction to what came before

People who seek love in urinals deserve our attention

I spend my days lying to myself in a storm of illusion

The blindfold had come off but my wrists still smarted

In my diary, I wrote, "Bitter constellations, tell me your names,"
    but no one answered

AVENUE X

I met you on the side of the mountain where there
   were no accolades, no colors

There were 2 mountains that we named A & B in our
   private language

Maybe I was your father among the stones in a different life

The sad part is growing old among smooth stones & mountains
   with names like A & B

The mountains were once underwater polished smooth like stones

We speed up as we drive through the falling rock zone on our
   way to the bottom of the canyon

I want to introduce you to A, she's my oldest friend

Ghosts are dead people who live in caves on the top of the mountain

Maybe people just die & that's the end

The two airplanes collided in mid-air but no one was injured

We drove into the mountains but when we got out of the car
   I thought I would faint

His heart began beating faster as he climbed down the side
   of the mountain

We construct a set for a play, 2 mountains (A & B), but the
   actors haven't memorized their lines

There's something about dying when you reach the top of the
    mountain & fall down

He didn't seem like the type who would lose consciousness
    at high altitudes

It's opening night & I still haven't learned my lines

We hang on for dear life as the train enters the city

I wear a patch over one eye to protect it from falling cinders

We talk in sign language, "A, this is B," as we climb the mountain

I rip up old newspapers & toss them into the fire

We climb the steps of the church in the old part of the city

From here, we can see the whole city, even the hotel
    where I used to stay

I used to think I could go to a city & be anonymous

I think I might write a letter to everyone I know & tell them
    I'm disappearing forever

The first scene of the play takes place in the foothills
    of mountain A

He flagged down a patrol car & asked to be taken to the nearest
    precinct

A white guy with long hair was accused of dumping her body
    in the alley

My apartment is where I go when I want to be alone

I put my tongue in her mouth & close my eyes

She took a photograph of his face while he was having an orgasm

There was someone taking photographs of us when we were
    making love, but I didn't know it

The cameras were rolling as we got into bed

The detective took photographs of us in bed together
    & sold them to my husband

Alone on stage, a monologue, on top of the mountain, catching
    my breath

In the opening scene, the two actors in the foothills of the mountain

I don't know how long I can survive in this blinding
    snowstorm, on top of the mountain

I wait until my anger builds up inside me & then I explode

The actor smashes a plate glass window with his fist
    as a way of expressing his anger but the woman
    just laughs

They find her body in the shelter of a cave on the side of the mountain

What remains is the spirit of her body in the shape of a tree

She returned to life in the body of an elephant or a pig

The actor stands on the side of the mountain & calls her name,
    but no one can hear

An echo of her voice down the canyon, a copy of her face in my mind

They accuse him of being a misogynist for cheating on his wife

The woman opened the door holding an ice pack against her eye

In the old days, we tried to reconcile opposing points of view,
  & create something new

The dream involved two mountain climbers, B & A, and two
  mountains

The problem is that there are only two mountains, A & B, as well
  as a body of water, which you can see from a distance

It seems like we better audition other actors and actresses
  who know how to memorize their lines

I can hear the bed creaking in the apartment above me at 4 AM

We have it on tape—the 2 people in the bed upstairs—which we
  play back to the woman's husband

The woman's husband claimed that he didn't care whether
  or not his wife had a lover & that on the night she was
  murdered he was in a bar watching television

It's important to have "seers" or "healers" who can distinguish
  what's real

My parents decided to name their first child after a flower,
  like iris or hyacinth

We showed the photographs of the woman & her lover
  to the woman's husband, but he didn't care

They called me "Lilac," but I changed my name to Marina when I was thirteen

When the fog cleared, I could see the granite peak of the mountain in the distance

"Calling" is a euphemism for sexual intercourse, as in "God called his woman" & she became pregnant, she became pregnant again

EYE CONTACT

We make eye contact across the crowded room
    but I'm too tired to speak

I write her a letter but at the last minute
    decide not to mail it

She writes in her diary how much she hates me—
    I shouldn't have read it

The Trojan War was a play put on for the pleasure
    of the gods

The Trojan War was produced by Zeus for his own pleasure

Deficient kidneys are often due to excessive loss of semen

Economic growth is promoted at the direct expense
    of human health

I saw you walking towards me from a distance but I lowered
    my eyes when we passed & you didn't say anything,
    you didn't say anything

The last time I saw her she was crossing Canal Street
    with her baby

Hold firmly to your goals, remain flexible in your methods

We met at a party & spent the next week in bed

We met at a bar, she told me her life story, & we never
    saw each other again

Every night, after the play, he gave the key to his hotel room
    to a different guy

Heard the one about the woman who left her car running
    while she went to the store & when she came back
    the car was gone, & her baby

Heard the one about the affluent teenagers who murdered
    their baby

You risk everything without thinking of the future
    or what you can gain

It's possible to take a risk, for its own sake, & not go crazy

You can speculate with the hope of gaining something
    which doesn't exist

"What you spit out falls back on you" — I copied that
    from a book

I copied some lines from Nietzsche & quoted them back to you
    but you weren't interested

I tried to impress her with my knowledge of Nietzsche, but
    she wasn't interested

They say you can't be happy unless you learn to forget
    but I remember every word everyone said, every time
    someone said something intentionally to hurt my
    feelings, or to retaliate for something I did

I begin telling her my problems but she interrupts me
    mid-sentence

He pulled the ski mask over his head & told the woman
    in the grocery to hand over her money

He threatened to kill the woman in the grocery if she didn't
    give him the money

We come from Korea, open a grocery, work our asses off —
    & look what happens

One day a guy with a ski mask & a gun came into the store
    & asked for money, but I didn't give it to him

I used to go to parties, sit in the corner, & wait
    for someone to talk to me

The body of the Korean woman was discovered behind the
    counter of her grocery

The teacher who was molested in the stairwell identified
    her attacker through a 1-way mirror

It's possible if you go to bed with your teacher you'll learn
    more than if you sit in a class with your hands folded:
    may I leave the room?

The student asked the teacher for permission to go
    to the bathroom & never returned

I stare at the woman across from me in the subway
    car but when she looks up from her book
    I turn away

It's one thing—to be aggressive—to go after what
    you think you want—& another thing—to sit back
    & wait for something to happen

The guy in the car behind me honks his horn
    because I'm going too slow

All I ever wanted to do was come to this country
    & open a grocery

The dog follows the scent of the animal into the clearing

We track down animals, skin them alive, & sell them
    to people who are hungry

I told the psychiatrist at the army inductee center
    that I didn't like women, & he believed me

A woman props her elbows on a cushion behind a screen

No one is to blame for your suffering but yourself

You can stand up, in the vertical position, until your head
    hovers above the skyline, or lie in your suburban
    sweat box until the branches begin to sway

We were two solitaries, eating alone in a crowded restaurant,
    staring at one another covertly above our plates

Even my words, now, this, copied from my own notebook,
    something someone else said, can't write her name
    without regret

She asked me what my intentions were, & I said: let's be
    friends

Sometimes it's best to be friends with someone, before falling
    in love

I go outside with a gun in my pocket like a petit bourgeois

They were loading their groceries into the back of their station wagon when a guy with a ski mask came up behind them & demanded their money

We met outside K-Mart & went for a coffee at Starbucks

Peyote poison presents symptoms similar to polio

Physical beauty & bodily health reflect good character

Because a lot of people say something, it must be right

Friendship is a response to the tragedy of love

Once the longing for a new world & for the tree of life seizes the heart, who knows what may come next

I can hear the sound of my voice saying something I already said

I stop to catch my breath where the road turns uphill

Resemblances proliferate in a swarm of analogies

The cop who stopped me for speeding wiped the sweat from his chin

POLYGRAPH

St. Francis received the stigmata in the diocese of Arezzo

"My sexual desire for one person lasts for about three years," she said, "and then I lose it"

There are spirits in the stones on the land where I was born

It's possible to go through life without saying "I love you" to anyone

There used to be horses in the barn but now there are only chickens & geese

The angle of reflection is equal to the angle of incidence

We lived for a few months in a house overlooking the ocean

The water from the well is infected with mosquitoes

I told a few lies this week, but didn't hurt anyone's feelings

A fly settles on the cap of a bottle of hand lotion

A man with red hair was arrested for strangling middle-aged women with their stockings

Take the syllable as heartbeat & press your ear to the pavement

My ancestors were buried in a clearing behind the barn

The death rate of blacks who worked on the Panama Canal was three times as high as whites

I respond to what you say by banging my head against the wall

We live on the same land where our parents were born, & their
    parents before them

The only time my mother touched me is when she hit me

I went to my grandmother's apartment on East 18th Street
    in Manhattan, I stood under the Third Avenue El

The bartender poured him a drink & he stared at it without longing

There's a woman who sleeps with the man with red hair without
    realizing that he's the person who murdered her
    best friend

He appeared in my dream in the shape of a giant penis

I can't imagine sitting in a bar alone & not smoking

There's a giant penis growing in the clearing behind the house

Sexual intercourse between colonizing men & native women
    is not uncommon

There was a sign posted on the back door warning strangers
    of locusts & wasps

We drove up the Palisades to a park overlooking the Hudson,
    I've been here before

My parents, & their parents, are buried in the clearing behind the barn

My worst self expresses itself when you least expect it

I have to warn you, my worst self is in ascendance these days,
    it must be the weather

Any day now, my worst self is going to rear its ugly head

"If not for each other we should be occupied only with ourselves"

I put on a good face in an attempt to hide my ugly self

I was here before, with you, it seems like yesterday, & then it ended

I saw you cross the street out of the corner of my eye but
    by the time I parked the car you had disappeared

Some mornings cold soup makes a natural environment

Prescience is the knowledge of things that may come to pass

The grasshopper sings all summer & mocks the drudgery of the ant

Some men with masks came to our house late at night
    & told us to leave

I smile in a feeble attempt to hide my anger

It's winter again & the grasshopper has no food

It's winter: the grasshopper is begging the ant for food

The red haired guy at the bar asked me back to his apartment, but
    I didn't go

I can hear your voice, from twenty years ago, calling my name
    from the other room

No one was surprised when the janitor found her body
    on the floor of her cell

There was the story about the grasshopper who played all summer
    while the ant worked so it would have food for the winter &
    then when winter came the grasshopper had to beg
    the ant for food

Some gods who were locked in a cage of their own making
    were released without warning into the custody
    of their immediate family

"If you look at the sun or some other luminous body
    & then shut your eyes you will see it again inside
    your eye for a long time"

La Reine, I thought, as she entered the room, & in my mind
    I bowed down

There was a diatribe in his head that might last as long
    as life lasts, that might go on forever

Describe relationship between "psychiatrist" & "patient" as "unhinged"

I replay a conversation with someone I haven't seen in twenty years

It was more than one could do to simply say "good riddance"
    or "goodbye"

The absence of passion is the key to longevity

Hercules cleaned the Aegean stables by diverting two rivers

Whoever loses his eyes leaves his soul in a dark prison

I hang on for dear life until the plane touches the ground

The bark of the tree is covered with mold & the stones
    that once were covered with miniature fields of moss
    have disappeared under water, like names out of the past

I quote out of context to impress you as we climb the stairs

The urethaned floor flattens out, cushioning my footsteps
    as I fall forward

I overturn a wastebasket on the living room rug & sweep it up
    with broom & shovel

The only person in my past I don't remember is myself

The people who work in the restaurant ignore us
    because we don't speak their language

A renovated tenement like back door desire through a hallway
    that connects

A HUNGER ARTIST

Connect dots to create a picture of something unimaginable

A woman, one of the women in the Bible, is walking across
    the desert

The sky is so close I can touch it with my fingers

I was holding an ice pack against the side of my mouth
    to contain the swelling

Old people with canes crowd the lobby of the nursing home

"It's been a long time," you say, & she says, "you haven't
    changed"

A mysterious lung infection was diagnosed by a doctor
    who was in love with his patient

Loving someone many years younger than yourself
    results in gum infection

Hardening of the arteries is attributed to loving someone
    who doesn't know you're alive

The star-crossed lovers limp down the highway with their thumbs
    in the air, but no one stops

A name that no longer designates a person's body

A name that no longer describes a body on a bed

Let those who underestimate me dissemble their own lies

We followed them around with a hand-held camera

We pointed the camera at the people undressing & climbing
    a ladder down the side of the pool

The sun is going down over the buildings across the river

The people with twisted smiles are heading home from their jobs

There are some people who actually pay us to follow them around
    & snap their pictures

Look into the present moment & see if your lover is beside you

A burning sensation above the ribcage—I guess I've worn out
    my welcome

It was the time of day when time stops & people take inventory
    of what they've done

Even the privacy of my diary is no longer adequate

Another fraction of an inch & the bullet would have penetrated
    his heart

"I'm not coming home tonight" (a message on a machine)

They add up columns of words & translate them into numbers

They study the Kaballah, the Zohar & the Pentateuch
    until the words eat into their flesh

Someone who objects to what we do, calling it an invasion of privacy,
    attempts to smash our cameras, but I manage to elude him

They build a boardwalk so the old people can sit in the sun,
   watching the half-naked people walk along the shoreline

After they left, I took a canoe into the center of the lake

After they left, I took a walk & ate some berries

After they left, I made lunch & sat on the porch

It was outside the precincts of the imagination that we came towards
   one another but without the brutality of two comets colliding
   light years from the farthest star that we disconnected the machinery
   linking the subtle arrangement of words & music & found ourselves
   careening through space at the speed of light

A young girl with torn fishnet stockings was sitting on the edge
   of the curb begging for money

The sun is going down over the abandoned factories

The people from the old country are sitting in the sun

Let's reenact—as in a play—the moment we first met

A dream of loneliness, a dream of being alone

A number that no longer designates a person or thing

I'll remember the clouds that changed shape in the beginning of
   summer, as you did, becoming a person I no longer knew

Nothing I say will make a difference

Stravinsky describes aging as "the ever shrinking perimeter
   of pleasure," & Marx said

"The only antidote to mental suffering is physical pain"

My sister's boyfriend sent her a letter written in blood

They operated on his brain & it turned out to be empty

A hunk, that's what they called him, as if he was a piece of cheese

Alternate side of the street parking regulations have been suspended due to religious holidays

There's a sinking feeling, as if I'm her, I put myself in her place—what I'd be feeling if I were her, if she had said the same thing to me

It was possible that I was happier than anyone who was living

Squirrels build tunnels & disappear into the depths of the earth

On the surface it looked like he was "going to pieces," but in fact he was the happiest person alive

Ruthlessness in emotional matters is always risky as far as possible after effects are concerned

He couldn't tell whether the woman in bed with him felt guilty because she was married

My father sits on the side of my bed in the darkness & tells me stories about a movie theater on Second Avenue where he used to spend his afternoons when he was younger & where an usher roamed the aisles with an aerosol can filled with insecticide

All I remember was that it was in a light like this one, late November, that you approached me with your bad haircut from

the end of a long corridor, & took my arm & lead me down the
steps of the hospital, through crowds of sailors suffering
from dementia

There were pictures of bodies on the walls of the caves

We see people dressed like animals fucking in the corridors

We shine our flashlights on the pictures of the animals
    on the walls of the cave

We lit a candle in the dark to see the bodies of the dead animals

There were people disguised as animals making love
    in the damp corridors

Expectation of things to come changes to direct perception
    when they're present, & direct perception changes to memory
    when they're gone

The Chinese waiter handed me a plate of sliced oranges

People go from one dependency to another in an attempt to prove
    their independence

The nature of the cure reveals the nature of the disease

Footsteps behind the door, the rustling of dead leaves

Traumatic experiences break through the protective shell

I stand at the door of your closet & touch the hem of your dress

She turns in her chair & for a moment I see a person
    I used to know

You produce a concept of what might be an image from real life

Loving without condition, a slip of the tongue between your legs

PIRATE RADIO

We can admit that there are some truths better left unspoken

An examination of fulfillment by means of self-denial

Hills in the distance, a single sentence

Solitude, not the same as solicitude

A fist opens, closes like a caress in the sun's shadow

A radio talk show host began to bark like a dog into a machine

I try not to pity him because his mother told him he would amount to nothing

I'm afraid there's no place within a hundred miles where you can get a drink after midnight

This will be interpreted by others as dichotomy—master/slave invective—but who can sleep?

I've been alive this long it seems I should know something but I don't

The woman on the phone said "If that's how you feel," & hung up

Think of the small talk that died when you were born

To all the poets who came before me all I can say is one thing

Property values fluctuate depending on the preponderance of predators

It's not necessary to follow someone to get to where you're going

The floor of the forest is covered with pine needles

Don't confess to crimes you didn't commit

Once I came up out of the white heat of day, & saw what others only dreamed

You were lying on your side with your back to me as I walked out the door

It's pointless to be alive if you have to work to make money

I beg you for small details so we can fill in the blanks

Perhaps rain fell like holy water in a forest, but you didn't hear it

The carcass of a barracuda washes up on the beach

We played spin-the-bottle & locked ourselves in the closet to kiss

Once I read *The Dead Sea Scrolls* in front of an open tomb & once I read *The Guide to the Perplexed* over lunch

Cup your elbows in lemon rind to get rid of wrinkles

It's pointless to be part of someone else's tradition

In this version, the guy who jumped overboard was given shelter by the inhabitants of the island; in another version, they ate him for lunch

Success at catching butterflies depends on the right territory for local varieties

The only tradition I want to be part of begins with me

You can't go back to where you thought you were without passing under the arc of forgiveness

The petroglyph of a fish on the wall of a cave

My mother stitched my name into the collar of my shirt

We wouldn't have slept together if we hadn't been drunk

We got into bed but we were too drunk to fuck

The movie opens with a shot of the gangster in bed with his girlfriend

There's the story about the gangster who had to murder his girlfriend because she threatened to go to the police

Time passes, people change, my closest friend is now a stranger

Estrangement is distance: separation from self, separation from others

One moment you were here, within shouting distance; now you're gone, changing shape like a cloud

A boat lost at sea on the edge of the horizon

On the last day of class, the student embraces me

It seems like someone was pushed overboard when no one was looking

It happened so long ago I can no longer remember it (a new version of necrophilia with the bad parts erased)

Offer your body to a stranger & see what happens

Everywhere you look it's Autumn at 3 AM

There's an argument among the heretics about who's going to die first

A view of the river & the tugboats (touching dry land), a photograph of Anna Akmatova as a child

Off-hand, sleight of hand, reprimand: keeping him on the hook

I thought I knew you but it was as if you had changed overnight

A new transplant victim was embalmed on a gurney

A latchkey kid sits alone in his basement

If you're too frightened to look up, look down (look askance)

I took it for granted that I knew what she was thinking

Waiters in cummerbunds hold forth on the plight of the pharmaceutical industry & the preponderance of dentistry candidates
at leading colleges

I pronounced Mencius "Men-see-us" but she knew what I meant

If you'd like some company in the shower, I'm your guy

An intimate conversation that begins in silence & intimates nothing (fake charm)

The wings of a butterfly frozen in amber

I felt like I was burning out, but then I came back to life, in the metaphorical sense, or my interest in being alive returned,
& with a new vengeance

Sometimes it feels like we've been married for years & didn't know it

I thought I knew you but you changed & I stayed the same

You can measure your life by the things you deny doing simply by saying "it wasn't me"

One day we live on the top of Mt Olympus, the next day we're in Hades

Vivisection—mercury pump—organ transplant—dephlogisticated air (oxygen)—an inverted bell jar—birds

Consecutive words in sentences—death sentences, consecutive terms—sentence interrupted—

It's expected that people will be born with male or female bodies & that despite a lifetime of acts that compromise or even reverse normal sex role expectations, everyone will continue to live in the body of a man or a woman

We are not who we are or who we say we are—we stay the same— the farther we go—backwards—in poetry & love

THE ORIGIN OF THE WORLD

You want to know what it's like to be her when she isn't here

A moment of solitude to vent rage against desire

One of my legs is shorter than the other

I peed in a jar but someone was watching through a 1-way mirror

It's possible someone you don't know is hiding beneath your skin

It was a good day when we could play outdoors with our friends

It was a good day when the boy read *The Lives of the Saints*

They look at you strangely as if you were not them

Thinking "this is the way" I walk out into the sunlight

Thinking "this is the direction" I ask someone the way

We took a wrong turn & ended up in Hempstead

I went into a bar & asked for directions but no one would talk to me

Last year we could see straight down to the ocean floor

Last year, we stood on the shore throwing stones into the waves

Last year, driving home, a song on the radio, Clair de Lune

Her legs are crossed at the ankles & her neck is bare

They arrested the men who wore caps because they thought they were workers

They arrested the students & professors who were blocking the door to the lab

There were some dead mice in the cupboard when I moved into the apartment

There was a water beetle under the rug when I turned down the sheet

We take a taxi across the bridge with the city in the distance going up in flames

We deny the warnings & get caught in the storm

The character in the novel wants to know the etymology of the word lethargy

Some nights I feel too lethargic to hang up my clothes

I signed a letter protesting the arrest of the students

There's a song about a summer night when the two lovers meet, but no one's listening

The actor in the movie performs an autopsy on the body of the dead girl

They fished the body out of the East River & contacted her parents who claimed she had run away from home when she was fifteen

My parents lived together for fifty years

My parents moved twice in fifty years

My father used to swim in the East River when he was a kid

There's a scene in a movie by Rudy Burckhardt about kids jumping off a dock into the East River, but it wasn't my father

A party in the next room, everyone happy, but I'm alone

The arrests took place at dawn: everyone herded into the streets

It's hard to be alone when everyone else is having a good time

They came to arrest us at 6 in the morning but we escaped through the back window

You work unhappily towards a goal that will make you happy

It would seem like I was ordering you around but I was only asking if you could do me a favor, something simple, like going to the store for a container of milk or a wedge of cheese

They arrested the child who was hiding in the basement and herded him into the street among strangers & stray dogs who looked like they would eat anything, who hadn't eaten in days

There were dogs in the street, some of them limping, & an occasional cat darted over the cobblestones when the trucks rolled by carrying the people who were arrested

I create obstacles that lead me away from where I want to go

I receive an F on the final exam & have to repeat the course during the summer

The spirit of a dead shaman appears to me in a dream

I signed my name to the letter & the next morning I was arrested

I work all night, at a desk, without compensation

You can rent a whole house for the money I pay for this apartment

You were here for a moment, like a speck of dust on the edge of the horizon

You can always tell when a person was loved as a child

The roof of our house came off in the storm

I'd like to think it was possible to make amends for something that happened in the past

There are more ways to make money than going to a job every day

It looks like a cemetery with trees & flowers growing between the headstones

Inundation of the Nile coincided with the predawn appearance of Sirius

The most resolutely fragmented work can also be presented as the total work

You leave behind the house you lived in as a child

You leave behind your parents—they were never there anyway

You leave behind the neat tablecloth, the labels removed from cans & jars

"Depression," someone wrote, "is the hidden face of Narcissus"

I rushed forward into a world of bad endings & no forgiveness

I skimmed some money off the top & bought a car with a dented hood

Suicides are condemned to turn into trees

I stuck my hand in the penny jar & got six months in Danamora for shirking my duties as father, lover, friend

Joy disappearing without conviction on everyone's faces as they plunge into subway tunnel leaving their babies in the hands of strangers

He was standing in a doorway with the curse of beauty on his fingers

Desensitize yourself to the truth: it's never going to unravel

I made you the executor of my will, but you died before me

Writing the truth is different from living it

On the path of knowledge you might forget who you are, & fall in love

It was not as if you were in love but that you were thinking about love all the time & this knowledge of time passing was a way of existing inside a thought that seemed to stretch like a thread to infinity

It was easy to think that it was a kind of conspiracy, like in a play by Aristophanes, where the women get the leaders to do what they want by denying them sex, but in another sense it seemed like we were edging closer to a fascist state, the idea of dirty tricks, turning tricks, a movie of your life story shot backwards or upside down, so that the people making love seem to be hanging from the ceiling

I'm not so egotistical as to think that I might be capable of pleasing another person

I toss my jacket over the back of a chair & the chair disappears

Some words to look up: epitome, rescusitate

Easy to forget the debt of loving when it's gone around the bend

Twisted together, like an erotic tourniquet—a liberal tabloid with an anti-marriage sentiment—a sentient being with a tragic aura— c. 420 B.C.

THE SECRET POLICE

We joined the secret police so we could inform on our
    relatives & friends

We know the names of the books that our neighbors are
    reading, & the names of the people who visit

The woman in the apartment below us receives money
    for sexual favors

I overheard my mother & step-father talking about "guns"
    & called the police

The policeman directing traffic waves at me as I drive by

My wife's father's father was arrested for selling drugs to a minor

My father's uncle spent a year in jail for molesting young girls

I followed them down an alleyway between two buildings
    where a meeting was taking place & I wrote a report
    & sent it to my district officer

I have a key to the building across the street & all the apartments

I bribe the doorman of the building across the street
    to inform on the occupants, letting me know when
    someone has gone on vacation so I can ransack their
    apartment

In the bureau drawer in Madame R's bedroom, there was
    a passport in someone else's name

I told the police about the gypsies who beg for money
   on the street corner

With high powered binoculars, I can see Madame R receive her guests

The name of the head of the secret police is a secret, even to me

Every month someone calls me to give me my orders, the names
   of the people I'm to investigate & inform on

Once, when I was driving home, I saw the woman downstairs
   climb into the back of a van, with four men

We live in a neighborhood where it's common for women
   to solicit men for sex

There's a guy who sometimes sleeps in a doorway near the corner,
   but I won't give him any money

There are the uniformed policemen & women, who carry guns,
   & then there's the secret police who look like everyone else,
   but who also carry guns

I carry a revolver under my shirt, at the base of my spine

Once I had to investigate a priest & saw him in the apartment
   below, with the prostitute, could hear his voice as he
   offered her money—I have it on tape

I install a camera in Madame R's apartment so I can watch
   her undress before she goes to bed

Every week I write a report & send it to my supervisor

We have it on tape, the god-worker visiting the sex-worker,
   round about midnight

There's a meeting tonight, at the end of the alleyway, through
   a doorway, but they won't let me in

On the top of the bureau, in Madame R's apartment, I find a note
   about a shipment of guns

I inform my district officer that a shipment of guns
   is going to arrive on Saturday, February 1

My students tell me I look like Jeff Goldblum, the actor,
   but it isn't true

It seems like an anti-semetic perception — that I look like Jeff
   Goldblum — because we're both Jewish

When I asked my students what they were laughing about, Gloria
   said: "We think you look like Jeff Goldblum"

It occurred to me that some of my students have never seen
   any people who were Jewish except for me & Jeff Goldblum,
   but I can't imagine how that could be possible

In the same way that people say all black people look alike
   or all Chinese people look alike it's possible some people
   think all Jews look alike as well

People think they're flattering me when they tell me
   I look like Jeff Goldblum, but I feel hurt instead

There's a movie, starring Jeff Goldblum, about a man in the
   Middle East who's shipping guns to Israel

There was a rumor that Jeff Goldblum, or someone who looked
   like him, was importing guns from Rio de Janiero to Israel

My favorite Russian student told me she thought the Palestinians were all "animals"

In 1995, someone who looked like Jeff Goldblum, massacred 29 Arabs worshiping at the Tomb of the Patriarchs

"It was like a scene in a movie," someone said, "& this guy was the star"

I hire a bodyguard to "take a bullet" just in case anyone tries to assassinate me

The four-star general was last seen leaving the prostitute's apartment after midnight

My bodyguard waited in the hallway while I rifled through the drawers of Madame R's bedroom bureau

Photos of young men dressed up as girls were discovered in the bottom drawer of the general's bureau

There was a rumor that an undercover agent had infiltrated the organization which met once every other Thursday in an apartment at the end of the alley

There was a rumor that many of Bertolt Brecht's most famous plays were written by his girlfriends

It's possible to sign your name to something someone else has written

The paid assassin stood in a doorway outside the general's apartment

Even my best friends act nervous & shy when they're around me

I make contact with Agent V who tells me that a shipment of guns is arriving, but doesn't know when

An anonymous call, heavy breathing, no one answers when
    I say "hello"

I say "hello" in English & then I say "hello" in all the other languages
    I know, but no one answers

It seems like only yesterday that we were lying together
    on a blanket near the ocean

I take a ferry, alone, across the English Channel, in the middle
    of night

I was lying in bed with the curtains drawn, waiting for you
    to come

I see my body, pastel colors, on the floor of the ocean

I can hear the sound of the ocean through the open window

We're strangers now, but once we were lovers in a house
    near the ocean

We sit on rocks like sirens & wave to men in passing ships

We dress up like women & stretch our legs on the sand

We can see the ocean from above & the clouds passing
    in front of the sun

We go down to the ocean, after midnight, & take off our clothes

We fold our gloves on the edge of the horizon & preen
    on the hot sand

We stare at the sun, into the sun, through the light of the
 sun & the sun going down over the horizon until
 the boats on the edge of the horizon resemble brothels
 on wheels

We lie on a blanket near the ocean watching the sun
 disappear, islands of clouds dispersing on the horizon

This is the time I like best, late evening, when the sun
 disappears, & there are no secrets

Photo by Katt Lissard

Lewis Warsh is the author of two novels, *Agnes & Sally* and *A Free Man*; two books of stories, *Money Under the Table* and *Touch of the Whip*; three volumes of autobiographical writing; and over fifteen books of poetry. He is co-editor of *The Angel Hair Anthology*, published by Granary Books in 2001, and co-founder and publisher of United Artists Books. He has received grants from the National Endownment for the Arts, the New York Foundation for the Arts, and The Fund for Poetry, and is presently on the faculty of Long Island University in Brooklyn, New York.